Contemporary's
Essentials of Reading

Book 1

Wright Group

Photo and Art Credits

Computer art created by Jim Blanton; 3 (t)Gerard Photography, (tc)Matt Meadows, (c)file photo, (others)Doug Martin; 33 (t)Cynthia Johnson/Gamma-Liaison, (cl)Jonathan Kirn/Gamma-Liaison, (cr)Charles Sink/Gamma-Liaison, (b)Barry King/Gamma-Liaison; 42 (t)Matt Meadows, (tc)file photo, (c)Aaron Haupt, (bc)Gerard Photography, (b)Doug Martin; 43, 49, 57, 60 Aaron Haupt; 65 (tc)Aaron Haupt, (b)Larry Hamill, (others)Doug Martin; 72 (t)Matt Meadows, (tc)file photo, (c)Larry Hamill, (others)Doug Martin.

ISBN: 0-07-282260-0

Send all inquiries to:
Wright Group/McGraw-Hill
130 E. Randolph, Suite 400
Chicago, IL 60601

Printed in the United States of America.

5 6 7 8 9 10 079 09 08

The editorial staff wishes to gratefully acknowledge the contributions of the following advisors, reviewers, and writers, whose considerable efforts, suggestions, ideas, and insights helped to make this series a more valuable and viable learning tool.

Advisory Board for the *McGraw-Hill/Contemporary Essentials of Reading Series*

Dr. William Walker
Assistant Superintendent
Adult Basic Education
Knox County Schools
Knoxville, Tennessee

JoAnn Bukovich-Henderson
Director
Adult Education
SE Regional Resource Center
Juneau, Alaska

Nancy Wilson-Webb
Co-op Director
Adult Basic Education
Fort Worth ISD Consortium
Fort Worth, Texas

Reviewers

Connie J. Dodd
ABE Instructor
Frontier Central School District
Hamburg, New York

Julie Gerson
Coordinator
Goodwill Literacy Institute
Pittsburgh, Pennsylvania

Sandra Koehler
Director
Adult Learning Resource Center
Des Plaines, Illinois

Dr. Patricia Kuhel
English/Reading Facilitator
Labette Community College
Parsons, Kansas

Rubianna Porter
Director of Precollege Programs
Cleveland State Community
    College
Cleveland, Tennessee

Laura Weidner, Director
Applied Technology and
    Apprenticeship
Catonsville Community College
Catonsville, Maryland

Mary Jo Balisteri
Coordinator
Eastland Vocational School
Carroll, Ohio

Alice Whitenack
ABE/GED Instructor
Lane Community College
Eugene, Oregon

Book 1 Author

Dr. Nancy Burkhalter
Literacy and Language Instructor and Consultant
Laramie, Wyoming

Contributing Writers

Jean Lance
Program Coordinator
Ohio Family Literacy
   Statewide Initiative
Ohio Department of Education
Columbus, Ohio

Elizabeth Shupe
ABE/ESL Instructor
Right to Read of Weld County
Greeley, Colorado

Susan Paull McShane
Executive Director
Literacy Volunteers of America
   Charlottesville-Albemarle
Charlottesville, Virginia

Clarita D. Henderson
Educational Consultant
Buffalo, New York

Gail Rice
ABE Consultant/Writer
Palos Heights, Illinois

Laura Belgrave
Largo, Florida

Carole Gerber
Columbus, Ohio

Christina Hutzelman
Kettering, Ohio

Dr. Nora Ruth Roberts
Composition and Literature
   Instructor
Hunter College – Medgar Evers
   Affiliate of CUNY
New York, New York

Patricia Costello
ABE/ESL Instructor
San Francisco City College
San Francisco, California

Mary Frances Harper
Director of the Literacy Council of
   Grant County
Sheridan, Arkansas

Regan Oaks
Reading and Fine Arts
Columbus Public Schools
Columbus, Ohio

Erma Thompson
Developmental Studies Instructor
Dallas, Texas

Dea McAuliffe
Buffalo City Public Schools
Buffalo, New York

Rita Milios
Toledo, Ohio

Doug Hutzelman
Kettering, Ohio

Table of Contents

Family Life

Workplace Skills

Life and Basic Skills

A. Circle.

1. **A**   B   Ⓐ   C   Ⓐ   D   E   G   Ⓐ   P

2. **D**   D   B   E   B   D   H   J   D   F

3. **E**   R   F   H   E   I   E   F   E   H

4. **J**   P   J   I   L   H   B   Z   J   J

5. **L**   I   H   J   H   I   L   I   L   L

6. **c**   e   o   c   g   c   o   e   e   c

7. **t**   I   t   k   l   r   t   t   l   h

8. **g**   p   q   g   d   p   q   j   g   g

9. **2**   3   7   5   2   2   9   0   2   2

10. **6**   8   9   9   6   3   9   0   6   8

B. Match.

1.	B		H
2.	d		g
3.	a		B
4.	H		d
5.	g		a

C. Match.

1.	cat		was
2.	bed		cat
3.	tip		saw
4.	put		bed
5.	go		log
6.	was		tip
7.	log		put
8.	saw		go

D. Say.

1. of

2. shop

3. get

4. girl

5. put

6. the

7. pet

8. if

9. he

10. class

E. Match the signs.

1. stop sign

2. restroom symbol

3. quiet zone sign

4. school zone sign

5. yield sign

F. Read aloud.

1. Ann works.

2. She is in school.

3. She takes a bus.

4. She learns.

5. She reads.

6. She has children.

7. She smiles.

8. Ann smiles.

9. The boy is 8 years old.

10. The man eats eggs.

Alphabet

A. Trace. Say.

A A   B B   C C   D D   E E

F F   G G   H H   I I   J J

K K   L L   M M   N N   O O

P P   Q Q   R R   S S   T T

U U   V V   W W   X X   Y Y

Z Z

B. Read.

A	B	C	D	E
F	G	H	I	J
K	L	M	N	O
P	Q	R	S	T
U	V	W	X	Y
Z	a	b	c	d
e	f	g	h	i
j	k	l	m	n
o	p	q	r	s
t	u	v	w	x
y	z			

C. Copy.

A A____   B ____   C ____

D ____   E ____   F ____

G ____   H ____   I ____

J ____   K ____   L ____

M ____   N ____   O ____

P ____   Q ____   R ____

S ____   T ____   U ____

V ____   W ____   X ____

Y ____   Z ____

D. Write the alphabet.

Aa

E. Read.

a   b   c

d   e   f

g   h   i

j   k   l

m   n   o

p   q   r

s   t   u

v   w   x

y   z

F. Write.

a <u>a</u>   b ___   c ___   d ___

e ___   f ___   g ___   h ___

i ___   j ___   k ___   l ___

m ___   n ___   o ___   p ___

q ___   r ___   s ___   t ___

u ___   v ___   w ___   x ___

y ___   z ___

McGraw-Hill/Contemporary Essentials of Reading   Book 1

G. Follow the -------→. Write the missing letters.

A -------→ B -------→ C -------→ D

E -------→ __ -------→ G -------→ H

__ -------→ J -------→ __ -------→ L

__ -------→ __ -------→ O -------→ __

Q -------→ R -------→ S -------→ __

__ -------→ V -------→ W -------→ X

__ -------→ __

H. Follow the ‑‑‑‑‑‑‑‑→ **. Write the missing letters.**

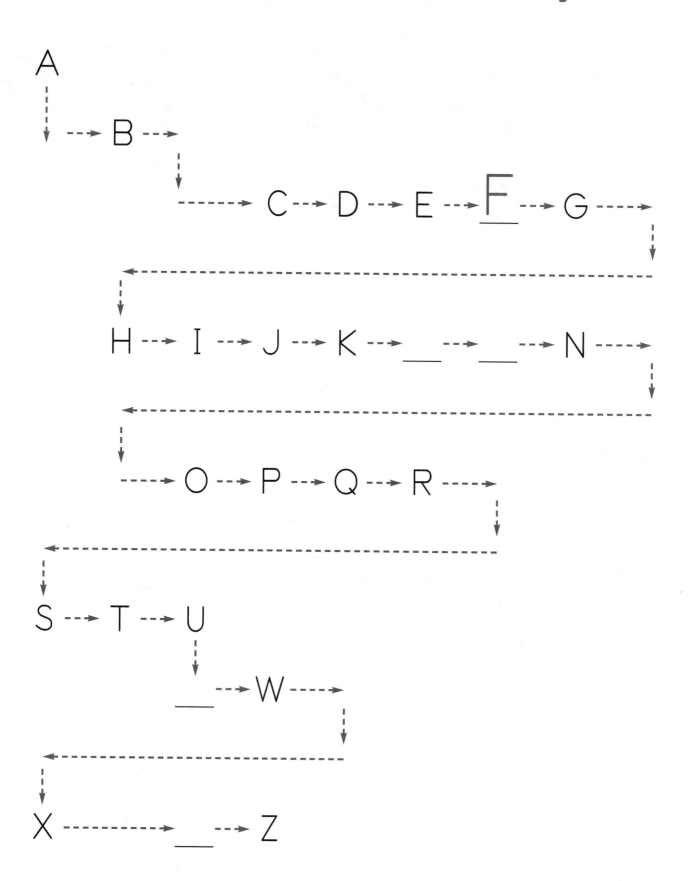

McGraw-Hill/Contemporary Essentials of Reading   Book 1

I. Match.

1. A   j

2. c   h

3. b   A

4. h   b

5. g   G

6. D   c

7. K   g

8. j   F

9. G   D

10. F   K

J. Circle.

1. A H (A) C X K (A) (A)

2. d b b d f p q d

3. C O D B C C R Q

4. h b p f h l b h

5. g p q g z p g q

6. D D B W B R C D

7. f t h f f b f h

8. j y p z q j p j

9. G C Q G P D G G

10. F P R Q F E F E

LESSON 2

Numbers

LIFE AND · BASIC SKILLS

A. Trace. Say.

1	_1_	2	_2_	3	_3_	4	_4_	5	_5_
6	_6_	7	_7_	8	_8_	9	_9_	10	_10_
11	_11_	12	_12_	13	_13_	14	_14_	15	_15_
16	_16_	17	_17_	18	_18_	19	_19_	20	_20_
30	_30_	40	_40_	50	_50_	60	_60_	70	_70_
80	_80_	90	_90_	100	_100_				

1,000	_1,000_
10,000	_10,000_

B. Write.

1 _____|_____   2 _____   3 _____

4 _____   5 _____   6 _____

7 _____   8 _____   9 _____

10 _____   11 _____   12 _____

13 _____   14 _____   15 _____

16 _____   17 _____   18 _____

19 _____   20 _____   30 _____

40 _____   50 _____   60 _____

70 _____   80 _____   90 _____

100 _____   1,000 _____   10,000 _____

C. Match.

	Left		Right
1.	14		16
2.	12		8
3.	7		90
4.	9		14
5.	16		4
6.	5		5
7.	3		7
8.	90		9
9.	8		3
10.	4		12

Review the Alphabet and Numbers

A. Circle.

1. E   R   T   H   (E)   P   (E)   F   (E)   H

2. **c**   e   o   c   g   c   o   c   e   p

3. **2**   4   5   9   4   2   6   3   2   2

4. **9**   8   9   1   7   6   9   6   0   3

5. **f**   h   t   f   k   f   r   b   h   f

B. Write.

1. A A   b __   C __

2. H __   f __   R __

3. O __   d __   L __

4. V __   g __   i __

5. Z __   p __   M __

C. Write.

1. 14 __14__   5 _____   9 _____

2. 8 _____   80 _____   1 _____

3. 11 _____   70 _____   7 _____

4. 100 _____   40 _____   4 _____

5. 200 _____   20 _____   2 _____

D. Follow the ------->. Write the missing numbers.

1. 1 --> 2 --> ___ --> 4 --> ___ --> 6

   ___ --> 8 --> ___ --> 10 --> ___

   12 --> 13 --> 14 --> ___ --> ___ --> 17

2. 10 --> 20 --> ___ --> 40 --> ___

   60 --> ___ --> 80 --> ___ --> ___

E. Follow the ------→. Write the missing letters.

A ---→ B ---→ C ---→ D ---→ E ---→ __

G ---→ H ---→ I ---→ __ ---→ __ ---→ L

M ---→ N ---→ O ---→ P ---→ Q ---→ R

__ ---→ __ ---→ U ---→ V ---→ __ ---→ X

__ ---→ __

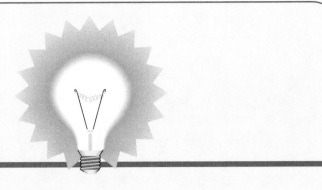

You Can
Name the Shapes

1. Circle

2. Rectangle

3. Triangle

4. Square

5. Octagon

6. Right arrow

7. Left arrow

8. Up arrow

9. Down arrow

10. Heart

LESSON 3

Consonants

The consonants are the letters:
b, c, d, f, g, h, j, k, l, m, n, p, q, r, s, t, v, w, x, y, z.

A. Circle b. **Boy starts with the b sound.**

1. (b)y   2. Bob   3. about   4. be

B. Write b.

1. __b__ ut   2. ____ oy   3. ____ een   4. A ____ e

C. Circle b sound words.

1. (box)   2. bat   3. dog   4. bus

D. Circle c. **Cat starts with the c sound.**

1. (c)ake   2. cap   3. can   4. cool

E. Write c.

1. ____ ane   2. ____ ape   3. ____ at   4. ____ all

F. Circle c sound words.

1. cap   2. cat   3. cot   4. cake

A. Circle d. **Dime starts with the d sound.**

1. do   2. dam   3. Dad   4. die

B. Write d.

1. ____ esk   2. ____ oes   3. ____ ime   4. ____ i ____

C. Circle d sound words.

1. dog   2. desk   3. dime   4. bike

D. Circle f. **Fan starts with the f sound.**

1. fee   2. foot   3. for   4. fix

E. Write f.

1. ____ ox   2. ____ un   3. ____ og   4. ____ ew

F. Circle f sound words.

1. food   2. hat   3. five   4. fish

A. Circle g. **Gate starts with the g sound.**

1. go   2. good   3. gum   4. gate

B. Write g.

1. ____ et   2. ____ oes   3. ____ ot   4. Me ____

C. Circle g sound words.

1. gum   2. gate   3. gun   4. girl

D. Circle h. House starts with the h sound.

1. he   2. his   3. her   4. have

E. Write h.

1. ____ al   2. ____ as   3. ____ ug   4. ____ og

F. Circle h sound words.

1. hat   2. house   3. box   4. hand

A. Circle j. **Jet starts with the j sound.**

1. joy   2. job   3. June   4. Jim

B. Write j.

1. _____ ar   2. _____ ust   3. _____ ack   4. _____ am

C. Circle j sound words.

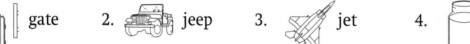

1. gate   2. jeep   3. jet   4. jar

D. Circle k. **Key starts with the k sound.**

1. kid   2. kiss   3. kind   4. fork

E. Write k.

1. bar _____   2. _____ eep   3. _____ ing   4. boo _____

F. Circle k sound words.

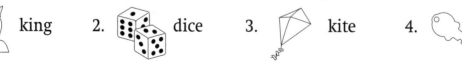

1. king   2. dice   3. kite   4. key

McGraw-Hill/Contemporary Essentials of Reading   Book 1

A. Circle l.  **Leg starts with the l sound.**

1. low   2. look   3. like   4. less

B. Write l.

1. _____ and   2. _____ ost   3. _____ ong   4. _____ ucy

C. Circle l sound words.

1. leaf   2. lady   3. lock   4. hare

D. Circle m. **Man starts with the m sound.**

1. me   2. my   3. made   4. met

E. Write m.

1. _____ ay   2. _____ ess   3. _____ ake   4. _____ ight

F. Circle m sound words.

1.  milk   2. money   3. heart   4. monkey

A. Circle n. **Nest starts with the n sound.**

1. no   2. now   3. nice   4. neat

B. Write n.

1. _____ ot   2. _____ ail   3. _____ eed   4. _____ ever

C. Circle n sound words.

1. nose   2. milk   3. nine   4. nest

D. Circle p. **Pan starts with the p sound.**

1. part   2. put   3. pull   4. pot

E. Write p.

1. _____ et   2. _____ ay   3. _____ oor   4. _____ a _____ er

F. Circle p sound words.

1. puppy   2. peapod   3. pan   4. pennies

McGraw-Hill/Contemporary Essentials of Reading   Book 1

A. Circle q. **Queen starts with the q sound.**

1. quit   2. quick   3. quilt   4. quiet

B. Write q.

1. _____ uinn   2. _____ uiet   3. _____ uarter   4. _____ uiz

C. Circle q sound words.

1. gate   2. quarter   3. queen   4. gum

D. Circle r. **Rabbit starts with the r sound.**

1. run   2. red   3. room   4. ran

E. Write r.

1. _____ ead   2. _____ ight   3. _____ ow   4. _____ ide

F. Circle r sound words.

1. ring   2. radio   3. ruler   4. watch

A. Circle s. **Sun starts with the s sound.**

1. so   2. soon   3. saw   4. set

B. Write s.

1. _____ ay   2. _____ uch   3. _____ ome   4. _____ ee

C. Circle s sound words.

1. six   2. socks   3. nine   4. seal

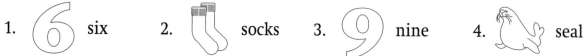

D. Circle t. **Truck starts with the t sound.**

1. take   2. top   3. took   4. time

E. Write t.

1. _____ ell   2. _____ ax   3. _____ ug   4. _____ ap

F. Circle t sound words.

1. house   2. truck   3. tree   4. table

A. Circle v. **Van starts with the v sound.**

1. very   2. vote   3. visit   4. never

B. Write v.

1. _____ al   2. _____ ice   3. _____ at   4. _____ an

C. Circle v sound words.

1. van   2.  bat   3. vest

D. Circle w. **Web starts with the w sound.**

1. we   2. wig   3. Walt   4. west

E. Write w.

1. _____ alk   2. _____ ay   3. _____ ell   4. _____ ish

F. Circle w sound words.

1. window   2. wing   3. ring

A. Circle x.

 X-ray starts with the x sound.

1. ax   2. X-ray   3. Tex   4. tax

B. Write x.

1. fi _____   2. wa _____   3. fa _____   4. Re _____

C. Circle x sound words.

1. ax   2. box   3. desk

D. Circle y.

 Yarn starts with the y sound.

1. yes   2. yet   3. yell   4. yard

E. Write y.

1. _____ ou   2. _____ our   3. _____ ear   4. _____ am

F. Circle y sound words.

1. yard   2. yo-yo   3. window

G. Circle z.

 Zipper starts with the z sound.

1. zoo   2. zone   3. zero   4. zip

H. Write z.

1. _____ oom   2. _____ oo   3. _____ one   4. Li _____

I. Circle z sound words.

1. zebra   2. seal   3. zero

A Closer Look at
Capital Letters

Names start with capital letters.

Ann, **Bill** , Carlos,

Dave, Eve, Fran, Grace, Hank,

Ida, June, Karl, Lee,

Michael , Nancy,

Olive, Pete, Quinn, Reggie ,

Sue, Ted, Ulrich, Vince,

Whitney , Xena,

Yanni, Zanna

Capital Letters

A B C D E F G H I J K L
M N O P Q R S T U V W X Y Z

A. Write or circle.

1. Write 5 capital letters. _____

2. Write your name. _____

3. Circle the capital letter in your name.

4. Write a name. _____

5. Circle the capital letter in the name.

B. Match letters to make names.

1. _____ ve   A

2. _____ arlos   B

3. _____ ill   C

4. _____ nn   D

5. _____ ave   E

LESSON 4

Short Vowels

The letters **a, e, i, o,** and **u**
can have a short vowel sound.

Short a   **Ax** has a **short a sound.**

A. Say the short a words.

1. at   2. as   3. an   4. and

B. Write the a for the short a sound.

1. b __a__ t   2. h ____ s   3. m ____ n

C. Say the short a words.

1. at   2. fat   3. am   4. Pam

5. ax   6. fax   7. an   8. fan

D. Circle the short a sound words.

1. (bat)   2. cake   3. apple

4. cat   5. candle   6. cap

Short e **Egg** has a **short e sound.**

A. Say the short e words.

1. beg   2. egg   3. less   4. best

B. Write the e for the short e sound.

1. l ___ g   2. M ___ g   3. ___ xit

C. Say the short e words.

1. egg   2. leg   3. sell   4. fell

5. best   6. rest   7. less   8. mess

D. Circle the short e sound words.

1. egg   2. eagle   3. seven

4. bell   5. nest   6. leg

Short i **Pin** has a **short i sound.**

A. Say the **short i** words.

1. it   2. in   3. if   4. is

B. Write the **i** for the **short i** sound.

1. k ____ t   2. f ____ ll   3. ____ f   4. b ____ t

C. Say the **short i** words.

1. it   2. sit   3. in   4. win

5. ink   6. mill   7. hit   8. bill

D. Circle the **short i sound** words.

1.   pin   2.   ice   3.   kitten

4.   pie   5.  pill   6.   milk

Short o **Mop has a short o sound.**

A. Say the **short o** words.

1. of   2. ox   3. on   4. mop

B. Write the **o** for the **short o** sound.

1. T ____ m   2. r ____ ck   3. b ____ x

C. Say the **short o** words.

1. mop   2. cop   3. Tom   4. Mom

5. ox   6. fox   7. rock   8. sock

D. Circle the **short o sound** words.

1. box   2. mop   3. boat

4. cot   5. top   6. 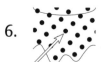 dot

Short u   **Cup** has a **short u sound.**

A. Say the **short u** words.

1. up   2. run   3. under   4. sub

B. Write the **u** for the **short u sound.**

1. c ____ p   2. s ____ n   3. t ____ b

C. Say the **short u** words.

1. up   2. cup   3. sub   4. rub

5. under   6. thunder   7. run   8. fun

D. Circle the **short u sound** words.

1. gun   2. cup   3. umbrella

4. sun   5. tube   6. tub

Word Families

A. Write **short a** words in the circles.
   Use the letters **c, f, m,** and **p.**

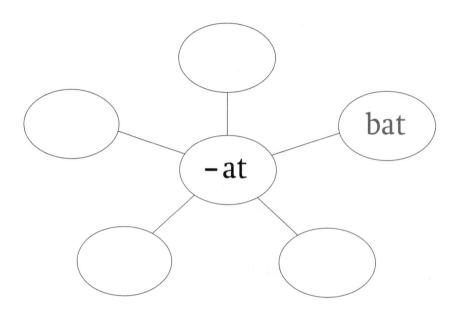

B. Write **short e** words in the circles.
   Use the letters **f, w, s,** and **t.**

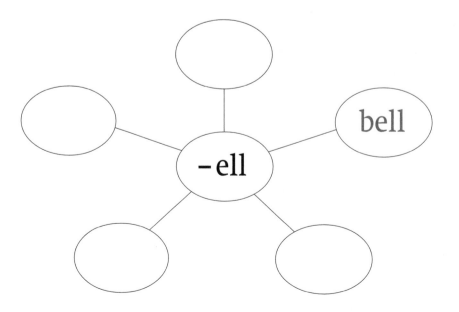

C. Write **short i** words in the circles.
Use the letters **b, f, g, h, k,** and **m.**

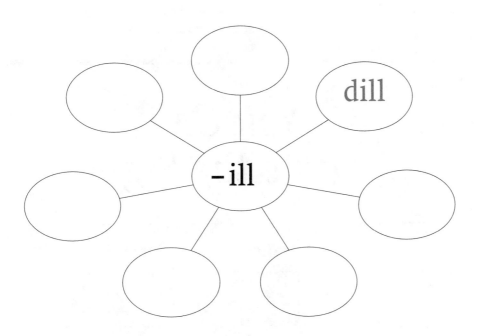

D. Write **short u** words in the circles.
Use the letters **b, d, m,** and **r.**

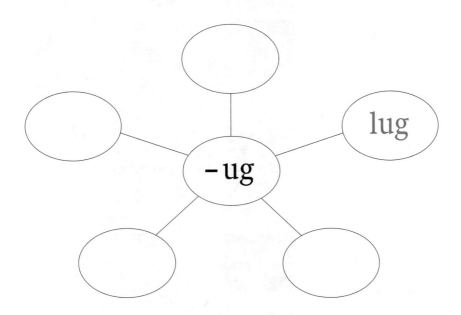

You Can
Name the Signs

	Sign	Name
1.		stop sign
2.		_____
3.		_____
4.		_____
5.		_____

Letters, Sounds, and Words

A Story for You

FAMILY LIFE

This Is Ann

Ann is a student.

She is in night school.

Ann takes a bus to school.

She learns the letters.

Ann learns the numbers.

She learns to write.

Ann reads every day.

Word Families

A. Write the letter A or a.

1. $\underline{\text{A}}$ nn   2. _____ t   3. _____ ll   4. _____ m

B. Add the letter to the word an.

r + an =   ran

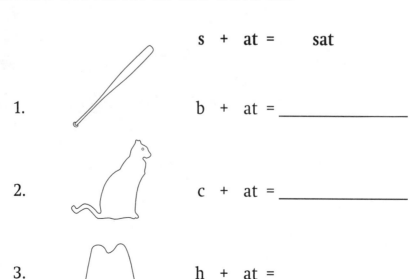

1.   f + an = _____

2.   m + an = _____

3.   p + an = _____

C. Add the letter to the word at.

s + at =   sat

1.   b + at = _____

2.   c + at = _____

3.   h + at = _____

McGraw-Hill/Contemporary Essentials of Reading   Book 1

D. Add the letter to the word all.

b + all = ball ◯

1. f + all = _____

2. w + all = _____

3. t + all = _____

4. c + all = _____

5. m + all = _____

E. Add the letter to the word am.

h + am = ham

1. S + am = _____

2. r + am = _____

3. j + am = _____

4. t + am = _____

F. Read.

Sam likes jam.

G. Write.

Sam likes jam. _____

H. Make a family of **and** words.
Use the letters **b, h, l, and s.**

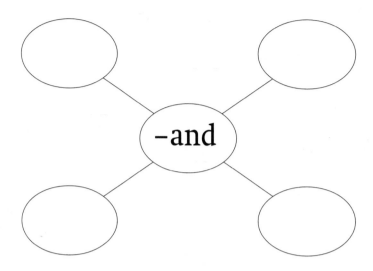

-and

I. Circle **S** or **s.**

1. sun   2. school   3. bus

4. Sandra   5. she   6. Saturday

J. Write words with **A** or **a.**

Ann _____

_____

K. Write words with **B** or **b.**

_____

L. Write words with **C** or **c.**

_____

M. Write.

1. My name is _____.

2. I go to _____.

3. I learn _____.

A Closer Look at Time

A. Look at the clock.

B. What time is it?

_____ 9:00 o'clock

C. Look at the clocks below.

1. Which clock says 7 o'clock? _____

2. Which clock says 12 o'clock? _____

3. Which clock says 3 o'clock? _____

4. Which clock says 4 o'clock? _____

A.

B.

C.

D.

A. Read.

Ann gets up at 7:00 A.M.

B. Write.

I get up at _____.

C. Put in the time.

1.   8:00

2.   12:00

3.   2:00

4.   6:00

LESSON 6

Long Vowels

A Story for You

FAMILY LIFE

Meet Bob

Bob is his name.

He is a nice man.

He is a teacher.

He teaches Ann.

Bob teaches reading.

Ann likes him.

He smiles.

Bob has one leg.

He sits in a wheelchair.

Word Families

The letters a, e, i, o, and u can have a long vowel sound

Long A 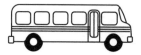 The *a* in **face** says its name.

A. Write a.

1. l ____ te   2. m ____ ke   3. n ____ me   4. d ____ y

B. Say. Listen to the A sound.

1.   late ⟶ **Now say** ⟶ rate.

2.   make ⟶ **Now say** ⟶ take.

3.   name ⟶ **Now say** ⟶ same.

4.   day ⟶ **Now say** ⟶ pay.

C. Read.

Bob is late.

D. Write.

Bob is late. _____

E. Circle.

1. Bob is (lake, like, late).

2. Bob will (make, take, lake) a bus.

50

Long E The *e* in **tree** says its name.

A. Write e.

1. k_____y   2. sh_____   3. m_____   4. w_____

B. Say. Listen to the E sound.

1.   tree ——→ **Now say** ——→ free.

2.   b**ee**t ——→ **Now say** ——→ f**ee**t.

3.   she ——→ **Now say** ——→ he.

4.   b**ee** ——→ **Now say** ——→ fee.

C. Read.

The tree is green.

D. Write.

The tree is green. _____

E. Circle.

1. The (fee, key, beet) fits the door.

2. We saw the (bee, green, beet) fly near the tree.

Long I The *i* in **kite** says its name.

A. Write i.

1. l ____ ke   2. m ____ le   3. m ____ ght   4. ____ ce

B. Say. Listen to the I sound.

1. like ⟶ **Now say** ⟶ bike.

2. mile ⟶ **Now say** ⟶ smile.

3. might⟶ **Now say** ⟶ fight.

4. ice ⟶ **Now say** ⟶ nice.

C. Read.

The dog might bite.

D. Write.

The dog might bite. _____

E. Circle.

1. Bob has a (kit, kite, bit).

2. Bob is at (might, fight, night) school.

Long O The *o* in **rose** says its name.

A. Write o.

1. b _____ ne   2. r _____ se   3. p _____ ke   4. _____ ld

B. Say. Listen to the O sound.

1.   bone ⟶ **Now say** ⟶ cone.

2.   rose ⟶ **Now say** ⟶ hose.

3.   poke ⟶ **Now say** ⟶ woke.

4.   old   ⟶ **Now say** ⟶ fold.

C. Read.

Bob is old.

D. Write.

Bob is old. _____

E. Circle.

1. Bob (woke, poked, folded) up.

2. Ann has a (bone, rose, old).

Long U

The *u* in **ruler** says its name.

A. Write **u**.

1. J____ne   2. c____be   3. ____se   4. c____te

B. Say. Listen to the U sound.

1.   June ⟶ Now say ⟶ t**u**ne.

2.   c**u**be ⟶ Now say ⟶ t**u**be.

3.   **u**se ⟶ Now say ⟶ f**u**se.

4.   c**u**te ⟶ Now say ⟶ m**u**te.

C. Read.

Bob likes that tune.

D. Write.

Bob likes that tune. _____

E. Circle.

1. Bob and (rose, June, tune) rode the bus.

2. Bob sings the (tone, tune, too).

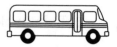

You Can
Name the Days

LIFE AND · BASIC SKILLS ·

There are 7 days in a week.

A.   Read.

B.   Write.

1.   Sunday

Sunday
_____

2.   Monday

_____

3.   Tuesday

_____

4.   Wednesday

_____

5.   Thursday

_____

6.   Friday

_____

7.   Saturday

_____

C. Write the letters.

1. Bob teaches on Mon ___ ___ ___.

2. Bob likes ___ ___ ___ urday best.

3. Bob rides the bus on F ___ ___ d ___ ___.

4. Ann eats fish on T ___ ___ s ___ ay.

5. I like _____ best.

D. Write a story.
Use the days in the week.
Write on the lines.

Ann is in school on _____. She went to the zoo on

_____. She took the bus on _____.

She eats eggs on _____. Her best day is _____.

Letters, Sounds, and Words

A Story for You

WORKPLACE · SKILLS

Ann at Work

Ann works.

She has a job.

She works in a pet shop.

Ann cleans cages.

She likes the dogs.

She likes the cats.

Word Families

A. Write e. Say the words.

1. p__t   2. g__t   3. s__t   4. m__t   5. b__t

B. Write b, j, l, n, and p.

1. __et   2. __et   3. __et   4. __et   5. __et

C. Read.

Ann has a cat.

D. Write.

Ann has a cat. _____

E. Circle.

1. Ann has a (pat, pit, pet).

2. Ann (bets, gets, pets) to work on the bus.

F. Write o. Say the words.

1. c__p   2. m__p   3. h__p   4. t__p   5. j__b

G. Write p, sh, st, fl, and cr.

1. __op   2. __op   3. __op   4. __op   5. __op

H. Read.

Ann likes her pets.

I. Write.

Ann likes her pets. _____

J. Circle the word.

1. Ann works in a pet (shop, top, stop).

2. Ann cleans with a (mop, stop, top).

K. Write short o words in the circles.
   Use the letters c, d, g, n, and p.

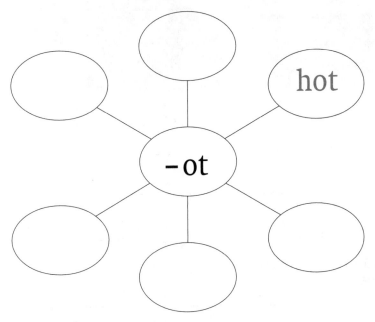

L. Write short a words in the circles.
   Use the letters b, c, D, f, and m.
   Write other short a words.

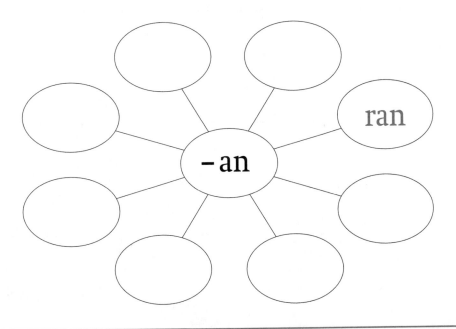

M. Read and write.

1. Ann takes a bus.

_____

2. Ann reads a book.

_____

3. Ann works in a pet shop.

_____

4. Ann likes the old cat.

_____

5. Ann has a dog.

_____

N. Write u. Say the words.

1. b___d   2. b___g   3. b___s   4. b___n   5. b___t

O. Write d, g, h, l, m, and r.

1. ___ate   2. ___ate   3. ___ate

4. ___ate   5. ___ate   6. ___ate

P. Read.

Ann was late.

Q. Write.

Ann was late. _____

R. Circle.

1. Ann got up (hate, late, gate).

2. Ann missed the (bus, bug, bud).

S. Write long a words in the circles.
Use the letters f, g, h, l, m, and r.

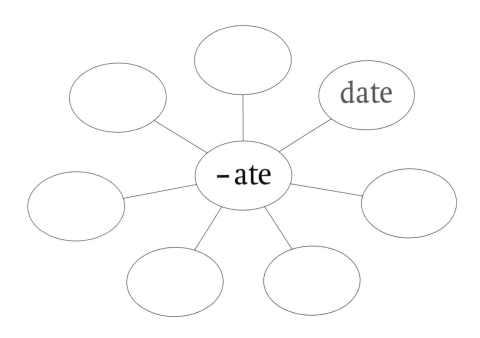

T. Read.

Ann gets up early.

Work starts at 8 A.M.

Ann got up late.

She takes the bus.

She was late for work.

U. Write a story.

Ann goes to _____ on Monday.

She likes_____.

She has children.

Their names are _____.

Ann is _____ years old.

She lives in _____.

She is _____.

Review

 Dog starts with the **d sound.**

A. Circle the d sound words.

1. dog   2. bus   3. did   4. dig

5. dust   6. up   7. day   8. big

 Girl starts with the **g sound.**

B. Circle the g sound words.

1. dog   2. got   3. late   4. quite

5. goes   6. gets   7. go   8. jog

 Top starts with the **t sound.**

C. Circle the t sound words.

1. dime   2. time   3. today   4. toy

5. tea   6. ham   7. at   8. pet

D. Listen for the **long i sound.**

1. life ⟶ **Now say** ⟶ wife.

2. five ⟶ **Now say** ⟶ dive.

3. night ⟶ **Now say** ⟶ fight.

4. like ⟶ **Now say** ⟶ hike.

5. ice ⟶ **Now say** ⟶ rice.

6. smile ⟶ **Now say** ⟶ file.

7. kite ⟶ **Now say** ⟶ bite.

5 **Five** starts with the **f sound.**

E. Circle the **f sound** words.

1. fire	2. file	3. gun	4. fun
5. her	6. fox	7. after	8. Friday

F. Circle.

1. **b**   d   f   b   b   t   h   b   k   b

2. **r**   e   r   o   e   r   r   s   a   r

3. **y**   g   j   z   y   q   y   p   p   y

4. **q**   p   g   g   q   y   j   p   y   q

5. **A**   D   B   H   A   W   X   A   B   A

6. **w**   y   u   v   w   u   x   w   u   w

LIFE AND
BASIC SKILLS

A Closer Look at Numbers and Signs

A. Say these numbers.

2, 7, 8, 9, 10, 12

B. Signs with numbers.

1.   Speed limit 45

2.   Will return at 3 o'clock

3.   Sign with fruit and price

4.    Highway route number

5.    City name with miles

Your Dictionary

Write words you met in this book.

A	B	C	D
an	ban	can	Dan
at	bat	cat	dig
all	ball	call	dog
___	___	___	___
___	___	___	___
___	___	___	___
___	___	___	___

E	F	G	H
egg	fan	gas	he
ear	fog	girl	his
exit	for	gum	her
___	___	___	___
___	___	___	___
___	___	___	___
___	___	___	___

Your Dictionary

Write words you met in this book.

I	J	K	L
it	jar	kid	leg
in	jet	kind	lad
is	jam	kiss	low
___	___	___	___
___	___	___	___
___	___	___	___
___	___	___	___

M	N	O	P
man	no	ox	pan
my	now	of	put
made	nest	on	pull
___	___	___	___
___	___	___	___
___	___	___	___
___	___	___	___

Your Dictionary

Write words you met in this book.

Q	R	S	T
quit	run	so	to
quiet	red	saw	take
queen	ran	see	tax
____	____	____	____
____	____	____	____
____	____	____	____

U	V	W	X
up	van	we	X-ray
under	very	why	
us	vote	wish	
____	____	____	____
____	____	____	____
____	____	____	____

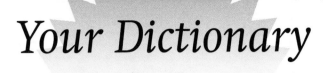

Your Dictionary

Write words you met in this book.

Y	Z
yes	zoo
yard	zip
yarn	zipper

_____ _____

_____ _____

_____ _____

_____ _____

Write words you know.

_____ _____ _____ _____

_____ _____ _____ _____

_____ _____ _____ _____

_____ _____ _____ _____

A. Circle.

1. **G**   B   G   C   G   D   E   G   A   Q

2. **E**   D   B   E   B   E   H   E   D   F

3. **M**   N   M   H   M   W   X   N   M   N

4. **O**   C   D   O   Q   B   O   Q   G   O

5. **I**   L   K   J   H   I   T   L   I   I

6. **e**   o   g   c   e   e   o   c   a   e

7. **k**   t   k   l   y   h   k   l   k   f

8. **q**   p   g   p   q   p   q   j   q   g

9. **3**   8   3   5   9   2   9   3   0   2

10. **6**   8   9   9   6   3   9   0   6   8

B. Match.

1. w   q

2. V   y

3. q   X

4. X   V

5. y   w

C. Match.

1.	was		fog
2.	eat		did
3.	fog		but
4.	hat		had
5.	see		hat
6.	did		eat
7.	but		see
8.	had		was

D. Say.

1.	to	2.	shop
3.	pet	4.	boy
5.	dog	6.	man
7.	bus	8.	with
9.	read	10.	job

E. Match the signs.

1. 45 miles speed limit

2. stop sign

3. school zone

4. restroom sign

5. city and mileage

F. Read aloud.

1. Bob works.

2. Bob has a wheelchair.

3. Bob takes a bus.

4. Ann learns.

5. She reads.

6. She smiles.

7. Ann likes dogs.

8. Bob works hard.

9. Ann is 28 years old.

10. Bob eats eggs.